Our Scars Matter

Edited By: Dana Hutchinson
Layout By: Shawn LeSuer

Library of Congress Cataloging – in – Publication Data: 2025945226
ISBN: 979-8-9880673-3-7

PRINTED IN THE UNITED STATES OF AMERICA

CONTENTS

PROLOGUE

Our Scars Matter is more than just a title; it is a call to listen, to understand, as well as a call to reflect and heal. In this book, five resilient African American women join me as we dive deep into the experiences we faced as a result of our health challenges. Our stories reveal not only our struggles with various diagnoses but also the emotional and systemic barriers that often go unnoticed.

My journey began with a revelation; many healthcare providers don't know the patient behind the statistics. But the amazing women who joined me in sharing some of the most intimate details of their medical conditions, are much more than a number! On a daily basis, we are juggling caregiving, maintaining our homes, meeting demanding deadlines at work, and fulfilling other family responsibilities, while often putting our health on the back burner. We have endured some of the most daunting challenges, from navigating insurance hurdles to confronting inequities in treatment. While our physical scars tell a story of what having an unwavering will and perseverance to survive look like; It's the invisible scars that are often hidden beneath layers of depression and uncertainty.

Writing this book was a personal endeavor for me. Following each chapter, I provide a safe space for the reader to reflect and write about their journey. After reading this book, my prayer is that the physicians who treat us as if we're just another medical record number, the nurses who lack compassion for us, and the hospital administrators who receive or turn us away from their medical facilities, will have a better understanding of what our scars really represent and say, "We see you and you are not alone."

ACKNOWLEDGMENTS

I thank God for saving my life and He is not finished with me yet. Without Him, this anthology would not have been written. He gave me purpose through my pain.

I would also like to thank my son, Dr. Maurice Champagne, who has been a constant source of strength; my mother, Juanita Champagne, who loves unconditionally; and my grandmother, the late Inez Jackson, who was and is still my guiding light from above.

To Chafica Miles, Ruth Harris, Michelle Brown, and Elena Crusoe Aiken, THANK YOU for sharing your heart and soul in the most amazing transparent and vulnerable way.

I can't thank the Board of Directors of my foundation, Open My Heart, enough for trusting and believing in this vision, and, of course, a heartfelt thanks to our supporters, whose dedication and support made this anthology possible.

Last but not least, I want to thank every reader who will buy this book. May these stories resonate with you, inspire you, and encourage you to advocate for your health. Always remember that your scars matter.

FOREWORD

In this uplifting book, *Our Scars Matter*, Dr. Florence Champagne and her colleagues will not only inspire the reader but also empower them. Through their compassionate dialogue, they share the victories they have achieved through their journeys with various medical diagnoses coupled with life's challenges. The symbolic use of the author's scars, will help the reader to see them as a "mark of courage." Although the stories center on their healthcare challenges, this book will also help those who seek to embrace their life's purpose.

The phenomenal women in this book are mothers, spouses, children, care-givers, employees, entrepreneurs, and more. They lay bare their experiences with grief and loss. Lessons on forgiveness and God's amazing grace are also a significant focal point.

They speak about the superwoman syndrome that often plagues Black women who feel they have to do it all with minimum support. This layering of roles is also referred to as the Sojourner Syndrome that's featured in an article by Professor Deborah Lekan (2009) that also addresses health disparities among African American women. Sojourner Syndrome was named after the legendary abolitionist and women's rights' leader Sojourner Truth, given her struggles against racial and gender inequality. The syndrome, "describes the multiple roles and social identities of African American women based on historical referents and adaptive behaviors that fostered survival and resilience under oppressive circumstances." Throughout the book, the authors share essential lessons about the importance of self-care, emphasizing the value of prioritizing oneself in the midst of responsibilities. They also offer tips that readers can use to ensure they care for themselves as they care for others.

A unique feature of this anthology is its emphasis on reader engagement through reflections and journaling. The authors encourage the reader to reflect on their unique experiences and provide space for them to jot down their thoughts.

The women are clear about the value of having a support system beyond their health challenges and take on their new purpose. They note that healing is inextricably linked to the support and encouragement of family, friends, faith communities, and organizations such as the Open My Heart Foundation.

Throughout the book, you will be introduced to African American cultural traditions that will both warm your heart and prompt you to reflect more deeply on cherished traditions and sage statements, such as "Right don't wrong nobody." Their testimonies will remind you of your own stories, which have been passed down by your ancestors and now have been placed in your hands to pass on to the next generation.

A theme that is woven throughout the author's personal narratives is health disparities that too often result in African American women being poorly served. Contemporary issues of social justice, such as reproductive rights and the lack of health insurance, are brought to light. Readers will learn about the importance of speaking up and the dangers of lowering their voices when confronted with systems that ignore their pain due to systemic inequalities. The collective message of the importance of self-advocacy is both compelling and resounding.

Sandra Edmonds Crewe, Ph.D., MSW, ACSW
Dean Emerita and Professor
Howard University's School of Social Work
Sojourner Truth Social and Racial Justice
Visiting Professor (2024-2025)
Rutgers University School of Social Work

Lekan D. (2009). Sojourner syndrome and health disparities in African American women. *ANS. Advances in nursing science, 32*(4), 307–321. https://doi.org/10.1097/ANS.0b013e3181bd994c

CHAPTER 1

BEYOND THE SURFACE – THE MARK WITHIN

BY CHAFICA MILES

Ok, let's talk about the obvious — my scar, the mark that runs almost the length of my torso. This incredible line represents the incision a surgeon had to make in the center of my chest, followed by cutting through my sternum and then separating the two halves to repair an atrial septal defect (ASD). I will always have this visual external scar but as we go through life, we experience many internal scars that can sometimes remain with us much longer and cause more damage than the scars we can physically see.

The Unseen Wound

As a single parent working full-time, I had a stressful job as an IT Project Manager that left me drained at times. As African American women, our nature is to be strong, holding down the family and hiding what is really going on in our lives. We know how to show our children and family that everything will be OK even when we feel that we have lost control.

There were many times I put on my "Super Mom" hat when I had to pick up my daughter from daycare and later from school. I did not want her to sense all the frustration, anxiety, and worries going on around in my head. I wanted her to feel excited, comfortable, and safe to share anything with me.

When my daughter was a toddler, I received a referral about a woman with good credentials who ran a home daycare. Everything started fine, but after a period, I noticed that my daughter would cry a lot when I dropped her off. At first, I thought it was just the normal detachment feeling a child has, but there was something more.

One day after bringing her home, I noticed red marks on her arms and legs. The daycare provider said she was probably allergic to something, but to me, it did not look like an allergic reaction. I immediately took her to the doctor, and I was unprepared for what happened next.

Social Services was contacted to investigate my daughter's condition and ruled it as abuse. The level of rage I felt was something I had never experienced before. I wanted to cause extreme harm to her daycare provider, but immediately came to my senses because what good would it have done for my daughter if I had ended up in jail? As if things couldn't have gotten any worse, by following proper protocol, Social Services had to investigate me as well. I could not believe it, especially after I acted on my gut feeling. Why would they investigate me?

I was subjected to scheduled visits at my home while Social Services observed how I cared for my daughter. I thank God that sexual abuse was ruled out, but unfortunately they did find evidence of physical abuse. The daycare was forced to close, and the owner was held liable. Trust and believe, how she was dealt with by the authorities pales in comparison to how I originally wanted to deal with her, but I had to let go and let God.

It has taken me a long time, with God's help, to move past this internal scar. I had to forgive myself as a mom for failing to protect my little girl and get over the shame I felt. Although she was too young to remember that traumatic experience, I held myself responsible for a long time, and it hurt badly! I also held a lot of feelings inside and away from my family and friends. It goes without saying the harmful impact the stress had on my body. I just didn't know the magnitude that it would have down the road.

REFLECTIONS

Have you ever held yourself responsible for something you had no control over? Did you forgive yourself? If not, why?

_____

_____

_____

_____

_____

_____

_____

_____

_____

_____

_____

_____

_____

_____

_____

_____

_____

_____

Too Young to Die

I was only 33 years old, and my daughter was the tender age of 6 on the day that I came home from work and started having chest pains and shortness of breath. I immediately went to the nearest emergency room and after being diagnosed, I was transferred to Georgetown University Hospital when I heard the following words come out of the doctor's mouth, "You have a hole in the upper chamber of your heart, an atrial septal defect (ASD), and you need to have emergency surgery."

Most congenital heart defects are detected during infancy or childhood, but I had lived 33 years with this hole. Over time, it grew larger and larger, but I had not experienced any symptoms. I never knew anyone in their early 30's who needed open heart surgery, and I cried because I could not grasp or comprehend how and why this was happening to me.

God had already brought me through so much before my daughter was born. I was sick during my pregnancy and after a long and painful C-section delivery, I came down with a fever twice and could not even touch her. I always tease her to this day, letting her know this is why she is an only child! Shortly after she was born, my marriage ended, and divorce proceedings started. I had the audacity to doubt the same God who had brought me through all of that, by saying, "You can't take me out now, I need to be here for my daughter and my family!"

It's funny how we have these conversations with God, questioning what He can and cannot do. When all He wants us to do is trust and obey Him and have mustard seed faith. I can't thank God enough for blessing me with such a strong supportive family, who stretched my faith, and kept me thinking positive.

REFLECTIONS

Write down a time when you questioned God. What challenges did you face and how did you overcome them?

_____

_____

_____

_____

_____

_____

_____

_____

_____

_____

_____

_____

_____

_____

_____

_____

_____

_____

_____

From Fear to Focus

Fear set in and my mind was going in a million different directions. I was thinking about how my little girl was just starting out in life and how I had pictured being there for every school trip, parent meeting, dance recital, prom and graduation. I also thought about how much I would miss my family gathered around the kitchen table telling stories and laughing hysterically about our beach vacations if I didn't make it.

In addition, three months prior to my surgery, I had just started my business as an Independent Wellness Consultant. I provided women an opportunity to de-stress with total body relaxation, impressed them with result-driven products, and how to spend less on products for their entire family. I was so excited to be an entrepreneur for the first time.

However, my fears started to subside when I focused less on my current situation and more on the life experiences I still wanted to enjoy and be a part of. A shift happened when I heard a soft whisper from God saying, "Trust me." It was the very thing I needed to be reminded of, and I could feel my fear transition to a level of comfort and my state of mind to be more at peace.

REFLECTIONS

Fear can take over when you least expect it and last longer than you want it to. What are some experiences you've had with fear and what are some of the ways you conquered your fears to help you move forward?

_____

_____

_____

_____

_____

_____

_____

_____

_____

_____

_____

_____

_____

_____

_____

_____

_____

_____

_____

_____

Out of the Mouths of Babes

I had my surgery in June of 1992, and my recovery period was approximately a little over two months. Remember back in the 90's, when technology was not as advanced as it is now? Shortly after my surgery I experienced pleurisy, which is inflammation of the lungs and chest cavities. I did not have to be readmitted to the hospital, but I required additional medication which resolved the problem.

My daughter was too young to visit me in the hospital and seeing me hooked up to tubes and machines but she was so happy to have me home. As I stepped out of the shower one evening, she ran into the bathroom to bring me a towel. When I opened the door all I heard was this scream of shock, "Mommy what did they do to you?" I did not realize what happened at first. I felt so good after enjoying my first shower at home since leaving the hospital. But now here I was standing in front of my baby girl in all my glory, looking like the "Bride of Frankenstein," sewn back together again!

The last thing a mother wants is to see pain and hurt in her child's eyes. I hated my scar because it was so ugly, dark, and it had just scared the heck out of my daughter. After she regained her composure from the initial shock, she looked at me, gave me the biggest hug and said, "I love you, Mommy!" At that point my scar was not so ugly and frightening anymore, I started to embrace it as a source of strength, because it represented "My Healing Line."

I prayed for God to heal me so I could be present with my daughter and family, and that is exactly what He did. Not only did God bring me through the surgery, but He also delivered me as I endured inflamed lungs post-surgery. My scar represented yet another battle He brought me through with grace and favor. It also stood as my right of passage that God granted to me – to continue serving as a mother, daughter, sister, friend; and to continue walking in my purpose that He designed for me.

REFLECTIONS

Sometimes a child can say or do something that makes you gain a new perspective on life. Has that ever happened to you? How did you feel before and how did the child make you feel after?

_____

_____

_____

_____

_____

_____

_____

_____

_____

_____

_____

_____

_____

_____

_____

_____

_____

_____

Never Stop Advocating for Your Health – Your Voice Matters

My heart was whole again and I knew that my cardiac challenges were over. It was going to be smooth sailing from here on in, so I thought. But 23 years after my first heart surgery I started to experience an irregular heartbeat. It felt like my heart was going to jump right out of my chest. I thought to myself, no way this could be happening again. I asked God to keep me around, but not to have my scar cut open again. I know that sounds ungrateful, but I was just keeping it real. Truthfully, I was so scared. Sometimes, remembering what God has already done escapes our memory.

Between the time of my first and second heart surgery, my sister was diagnosed with breast cancer. Although she went through extensive treatment, she survived and is cancer free, praise God! As if what she and I endured wasn't enough, sadly my brother succumbed to a heart attack. Our family lost a wonderful man – a son, a sibling, and a devoted father. There are so many different ways the heart can be affected – physically, emotionally and spiritually.

This time I had different doctors and when I first expressed concern about my abnormal heartbeat, it was not addressed as urgently as I would have liked. The doctors prescribed several medications. But unfortunately, one of them did not provide any noticeable relief and the other one made me sick after taking it repeatedly. It had only been out on the market for less than two years, and usually that is not enough time to determine all of the side effects. Finally, I had to speak up, voice my concerns, and take control of my teatment plan.

This happens a lot with women, especially African American women whose symptoms and pain are more apt to be downplayed or misdiagnosed. But not this woman! I guess they did not know who they were messing with. I am the proud daughter of the first African American female pharmacist in my hometown, and my mother did not play. I requested a consultation with the doctor, made my concerns known, and with the help of my "don't play with me" momma, I was scheduled for a cardiac ablation in January 2015.

Understand that every heart surgery is serious, but the cardiac ablation was not nearly as extensive as my first surgery and did not involve cutting through my sternum again. Rather, it involved modifying and destroying the tissue around my heart that caused my abnormal heart rhythm. After my procedure, my heart returned to beating at a normal, healthy rate and I truly felt like a new woman. When it comes to your body, you should never lower your voice to blend in or keep quiet to avoid advocating for your health by challenging medical professionals who are deemed experts.

REFLECTIONS

Was there a time in your life when you either wanted to speak up, or you did speak up, but your voice was not heard, and you were shut down or overlooked? How did it make you feel and what did you learn from it that empowered you to handle future situations?

_____

_____

_____

_____

_____

_____

_____

_____

_____

_____

_____

_____

_____

_____

_____

_____

_____

Whispers from a Scar

Not all scars are born from something tragic. Some of them are the result of something comical. After you get over the pain somehow you find humor in the situation. Do you have a scar that reminds you of something funny? If so, most likely it happened because you were doing something you had no business doing. It may cause people to whisper, "Now how in the world did she get that?"

We all have stories from our childhood scars, and this is one of my favorites. I loved hanging out with my brother because he was always coming up with the wildest things. My mom was a single parent raising the three of us and sometimes worked in the evening. However, my sister was the oldest and had to watch us from time to time.

One evening when she was washing clothes, the washing machine overflowed. Instead of immediately cleaning up the water, my brother had the bright idea of turning it into an Olympic sport and suggested we slide down the hallway in it. I agreed, slid, and fell, hitting my chin, only to get up and keep going. While my brother and sister were screaming, unbeknownst to me I had busted a hole in my chin and had to go to the hospital where I received stitches. You can imagine what happened to all of us once my mom returned home. To me it was a mark of courage, and it was worth it!

Another memorable scar story was when I brought a nice pair of cuffed pants to wear to an event. I put them on and yes, I was feeling myself because they fit so well and I looked fabulous! Of course I was in a rush and decided to put my heels on before I went down the stairs to save time.

Well as you probably guessed, as I was going down the stairs, my heel got caught in my cuff and I fell all the way down to the bottom. I had to have surgery on my ankle for a torn ligament and to remove bone fragments. Now, it did take me a while to laugh about this one, but to this day I carry my shoes with me while going down the steps. Lesson learned!

REFLECTIONS

What is your "what was I thinking" scar? How did you get it, and do you still have that scar today?

_____

_____

_____

_____

_____

_____

_____

_____

_____

_____

_____

_____

_____

_____

_____

_____

Finding Beauty in Brokenness

I understand now more than ever that the journey God had to take me on was so my heart would be strong enough to carry out His plan and purpose for me. I learned a lot about my body — what it needed and when to rest. But the two biggest lessons were how to say no and how to ask for help.

It was not by accident that God guided me on this path three months after I started my wellness business. How could I pamper and teach the importance of self-care to women when I did not practice it myself. I was still angry and hurt from my divorce, afraid of being a single parent, and stressed out on my job. But that one evening in 1992 when I started having pains in my chest and shortness of breath, I had to be put in "time out," because I was determined to do things on my own.

During my recovery, I had no choice but to sit back and look beyond the surface of my scar and reflect on everything that happened, the effect it had on me, and how it changed me. I also questioned if I should have started my business, but once again God answered that question. While I was recuperating, my friends came by to visit to make sure I was still alive, and they had another purpose in mind as well. They loved how my wellness products made them look and feel and wanted more!

REFLECTIONS

What do you believe is God's purpose for your life? Are you working on your purpose now? If not, what support do you need to achieve your goals?

_____

_____

_____

_____

_____

_____

_____

_____

_____

_____

_____

_____

_____

_____

_____

_____

_____

_____

My Healing Line

I now feel empowered and definitely equipped to share with women about the dangers of heart disease. Early detection is key! I could have disregarded my shortness of breath, chalked it up to just being tired, and continued to fix dinner, help my daughter get ready for bed, and prepare for another day of work.

It's not called a woman's intuition for nothing. When you feel deep down inside something is wrong with your body and you need to address it, don't put it off until you have time to fit it in, or because you don't want to bother someone. It should be addressed immediately! Our continual never-ending to-do-list is usually missing something very important at the top, OUR NAME!

My scar, or as I call it, "My Healing Line," has changed me not because of its physical appearance, but because I have an emotional connection to women like me who struggle silently with the daily hectic pace of life, trying to make ends meet. I am very proud of my spiritual growth regarding forgiveness, trust, and faith in God to let go of things I have no control over.

Today, I create wonderful relaxation experiences for women and their families to escape from life's everyday challenges and demands. The wonderful client testimonies and the many "thank you" messages I receive for helping women renew their commitment to self-care, strengthens my commitment to make a difference in their lives.

Since 2019 I have supported the Open My Heart Foundation and their mission to eliminate heart health disparities among African American women and other women of color. As one of the recipients of the "Survivor That Thrives" award in 2022, I continue to share my story to make women aware of heart disease.

REFLECTIONS

Do you follow a self-care regimen? How often do you take time out for yourself? If not, what would it take for you to implement a self-care routine in your weekly activities?

_____

_____

_____

_____

_____

_____

_____

_____

_____

_____

_____

_____

_____

_____

_____

_____

_____

_____

_____

Chafica's Six Self-Care Tips

Create your own personal oasis. Find a room, chair, your backyard, or any space where you can surround yourself with items that bring you comfort and peace to seek prayer or stillness. What is your favorite place to just be still? What items do you have around you that bring you joy?

Enlighten your mind. Gather family/friends together and relive conversations, pictures, and videos of wonderful experiences and joyful times. What is one of your favorite family gatherings? What are some of your memories that bring you joy and peace?

Give yourself a daily dose of laughter. Everyone needs a laughing buddy (LB) to fill their soul with happiness. Who are your top 3 LBs you can call anytime to fill your heart with joy? Why are they special to you?

Mix up your day with music. Release, let go, and dance to your favorite song; or close your eyes and escape with sounds of tranquility and joy. What are a couple of your favorite songs to just let go and dance to? What memories do the songs bring back to your remembrance?

Dare to do YOU! Rejuvenate your body with a nice massage, stir your spirit with aromatic scents, and dazzle yourself with whatever makes you feel and look great. What is one of your favorite outfits that makes you feel great, and you know you look fabulous?

Smile and pay it forward. Share these steps to have a positive influence on someone's life. Who are 3 people you would like to share these self-care tips with? Why do you think they would benefit from them?

Bio

Chafica Miles

Chafica Miles is a Springfield, Massachusetts native who currently resides in Maryland. She is an independent Skin Care/Spa Consultant and District Leader with JAFRA Cosmetics International, where she serves as a coach and speaker.

She is a published author and a certified Color Match Specialist. Chafica earned an Associates of Arts degree in Computer Science as well as a Bachelor of Science degree in Project Management, using her skills and talents to provide marketing/proposal consulting services.

Chafica loves to bring girlfriends, mothers and daughters, and husbands and wives together to create a renewed commitment to self-care. She is the proud mother of an amazing daughter who is a licensed cosmetologist.

To connect with Chafica:

Email: Chafica.miles@gmail.com
Website: www.Jafra.com/cmiles
Cell: 240-513-8823
Facebook: Chafica's Self-Care

CHAPTER 2

'TIL DEATH DO US PART

BY RUTH HARRIS

On January 6, 2021, there was a major event that occurred in Washington, D.C., the insurrection of the United States Capitol. While most people will never forget what they were doing on that day, it's a day that I will never forget for another reason. A life-altering event happened to me; I had a heart attack.

I have been on a plant-based diet for 55 years. I exercise regularly, I take my vitamins, and I love walking. I've done and continue to do everything that I am expected to do to maintain a healthy lifestyle. But even with all of that, I never imagined that I would have a heart attack. In retrospect, it was the stress that got me. I was a caregiver for my husband for 10 years.

Initially, he was diagnosed with dementia, and then Alzheimer's Disease, which got progressively worse. In addition, over time, he had six strokes. I was suddenly faced with mounting responsibilities such as transporting him back and forth to doctors' appointments for swallowing tests, breathing tests, and sleep studies. This was in addition to cooking, shopping, meal prepping, coordinating home care, making accessibility changes in the house, you name it.

It wasn't easy. At times, I had to fight back and forth with insurance providers, to ensure that he got the care and help that he needed to have a decent quality of life. I did everything within my power to provide exceptional care for my husband. However, what I did not realize was the stress, the strain, and the wear and tear that it was causing me. By me having lived such a healthy lifestyle, I could not fathom why this was happening to me, but my doctor confirmed what I already knew, my heart attack was stress-induced.

I went from taking zero medications to seven different ones. I learned that you can be a vegan, a vegetarian, or adopt any other healthy diet of your choice; but stress, aka the "silent killer," can take you in another direction, in spite of being health conscious.

It was my wifely duty to make everything more comfortable for my husband. After all, we took the vow, in sickness and in health, so as far as he was concerned, there was nobody else responsible for caring for him but me. It was a struggle to get everything done each day. I was not thinking about myself at all. During his decline, all I could think about was his quality of life and what more I could do to help him.

REFLECTIONS

Have you ever felt that you needed to do everything for someone else, a job, or a situation, and neglected to care for yourself in the process? If so, how did it impact your way of life, health, stress level, etc.?

_____

_____

_____

_____

_____

_____

_____

_____

_____

_____

_____

_____

_____

_____

_____

_____

_____

Put Your Mask on First

As a former airline flight attendant, there's a part of the safety briefing when we explain and demonstrate to the passengers, that if the cabin loses air pressure, the masks will automatically fall and they'll have to put them on themselves first, before helping someone else, even if they have a small child traveling with them.

One might think that it should be self-evident, right? But in an actual emergency, sometimes adrenaline kicks in, especially when a parent is traveling with a child and instinctively they will want to help them before helping themselves. However, in reality, as a caregiver, it's tough to face daily tasks alone without reliable support.

I have learned that self-care is critical and should be a priority. You're more effective when you have rested properly, take time for yourself, or visit with friends every now and again to avoid losing yourself in the process. Oftentimes, caregivers feel guilty when they do things for themselves when the person they're caring for is being taken care of by someone else; even if it's only for a few hours. You can't pour from an empty cup!

Prior to being a caregiver, I would schedule my annual checkups near my birthday. I strategically did it that way to easily remember each year. Here are some other invaluable tips that I have learned and adopted in my self-care regimen:

When your loved one has a scheduled checkup, if possible schedule yours around the same time.

If your loved one has scheduled tests, again, schedule yours as well. It might be an eye exam, a stress test, sleep study, or a hearing test, etc.

No one can get to any place of significance by themselves. We all need support on some level. Research support groups or services for caregivers or consider connecting with a community of support systems that assist with the daily challenges that caregivers face.

REFLECTIONS

What are some things that you have learned to do for self-care, or ways to put the mask on yourself first?

_____

_____

_____

_____

_____

_____

_____

_____

_____

_____

_____

_____

_____

_____

_____

_____

_____

_____

_____

_____

The Diagnosis, The Purpose, and The Empowerment

Once I woke up in the ICU, the doctor and I talked about what happened and what caused my heart attack. I've seen actors on TV having one, and they immediately clutch their chest. However, that was not my case. Some of my symptoms were vomiting, tightening of the wrists, and lightheadedness.

I was diagnosed with a myocardial infarction, which is left-sided heart failure or a heart attack due to blockage in the arteries. The treatment options were either open-heart surgery or having stents put in to open the left chamber. I decided to have stents inserted.

After hearing the doctor's diagnosis and the treatment options, I chose to adhere to the doctor's advice, so that I could return to caring for my husband as quickly as possible. Even though the stress of doing so nearly killed me, I still felt that caring for him was top priority. This was the motivating factor to obey the doctor's orders.

Prior to having the heart attack, I previously went to a caregiver's organization, so that I could gain some insight into being a caregiver, accessing services, and getting the support that I needed. But after my ordeal, I felt that now it was me who needed support, the appropriate care, and special services. Approximately six months later, I was introduced to the Open My Heart Foundation (OMHF).

They hosted an All-Red Gala Event, where African American women and other women of color, who had heart attacks and strokes were being recognized and honored as "Survivors Who Thrive." I never thought of myself as a survivor and had never even used that term to describe me. But for the first time, I realized that in fact, I was one.

At the gala, I could not believe the amount of women who shared similar experiences regarding their cardiac journey. They were just like me, and I felt an immediate connection. This was the type of support I was missing. While attending the event, I felt empowered to also tell my story to help someone else. I discovered my purpose and found it through OMHF.

I began inquiring about becoming a member of this wonderful organization and joined. Through OMHF's support group, Supporting Our Sisters, I started connecting with other women, as well as obtaining resources, receiving heart health education from health professionals, and receiving opportunities to speak and to advocate for other women just like me.

26

Through this experience, I began to feel that my purpose was being fulfilled, and for the first time, I was connected to a sisterhood like never before.

The organization's CEO, Dr. Florence Champagne, shared with us why her fight was necessary. With heart disease being the leading cause of death in the United States, women especially are not screened for early detection. That alone was worth fighting for. But there was so much more. So she took her fight to the Maryland State Legislature and was instrumental in crafting the following legislation – House Bill 666 and Senate Bill 60 that would allow insurance providers to pay for Calcium Score Testing for early detection of heart disease.

The bills passed both the House and the Senate. The highlight for me was testifying before the Maryland House of Delegates, on the importance of passing this legislation. I was headed in the right direction.

When I gave my testimony, I believed it was and still is a cause that we all need to get behind and support, because it's no fun to wake up in the ICU having suffered a heart attack and not have the proper insurance or other necessities simply because you're a woman of color. I wanted to get in the fight with OMHF and all of the ladies that were there. I wanted to do whatever it took to support this powerful, powerful organization and their mission. I've experienced other organizations, but I did not feel that I was aligned with what they stood for, unlike the way I felt when I learned about OMHF. It was also important to me to join the fight because they were women of color and could identify with my struggles.

To my surprise, I was selected as a "Survivor Who Thrives" honoree at OMHF's 2025 All-Red Gala Awards Banquet. I felt like WOW; someone wants to hear my story and now it was me on the big screen encouraging attendees with my testimony. I was also invited to become a proud Board Member of this amazing organization.

REFLECTIONS

Have you ever found purpose and meaning, or felt empowered through a life-changing experience? If so, what was it, and how are you using it to empower others?

_____

_____

_____

_____

_____

_____

_____

_____

_____

_____

_____

_____

_____

_____

_____

_____

_____

_____

To Help or Not to Help

As I shared previously, after my heart attack, I just wanted to return to taking care of my husband. However, I did not realize that I also needed help, and that's when my daughter stepped in. She was living in New York at the time, and I was living in Washington, DC. Realizing the magnitude of what happened to me, she and her four children packed up and moved to DC to help me.

Not only did her assistance allow me to take a break from caregiving, but it also allowed me to get the cardiac rehab treatments that I needed to fully recover and get back on my feet. It also helped to relieve stress as I healed.

Her presence and assistance taught me that it's okay to ask for help. However, as my husband's caregiver, I vowed not to ask for help mainly because of a past experience where I had been let down by someone who said that they were going to help me and didn't. I began feeling that family, loved ones, or those closest to you were the ones who let you down the most. As a result, I became hesitant to ask for help and decided that I'd rather do it all myself, or try to get services, rather than relying on others. Although others may not have intended to let me down, the impact of them going back on their word left a bad taste in my mouth. Therefore, I became a "one woman show" and developed the superwoman syndrome, thinking I could do it all.

REFLECTIONS

Has there ever been a situation where you were hesitant to ask for help due to previously being burned or lack of follow-through? If so, what was it and how did you handle it?

_____

_____

_____

_____

_____

_____

_____

_____

_____

_____

_____

_____

_____

_____

_____

_____

_____

_____

Community Healing

While I was living in New York City, I was introduced to "Readings," which are short stories presented to the public to determine if they garner enough interest to become a film. All of my friends were either actors, models, or production executives in the entertainment industry, so I either attended them or accompanied my friends often.

These readings produced lots of famous people in "The Big Apple." By attending them, a seed was planted within me to tell my own story and that was the beginning of finding my joy.

It was during this time that I met my future husband. We had one daughter. He was in the advertising industry, and I was an event planner. As fate would have it, he managed the advertisements for the events that I was organizing. We became the perfect couple.

Since I was around so many famous people, I began to coordinate parties, large events, and eventually retreats. He began working at a bookstore and became an avid reader. Because he started having health issues, he began to read a lot about health and healing and became interested in attending health fairs and retreats. He would read about all of the health benefits of food, juices, and more. Even though patrons would come to read the books, he took it one step further by explaining the books to them. They loved listening to his knowledge so much that they started soliciting him for counseling and advice, so much so that he became well known in the community. He was renamed.

People came near and far seeking his health advice. Because of the many health issues that were plaguing members of the community, there was a constant flow of them looking for answers. As a result, we opened our own health food store. This eventually led us to start hosting health fairs and retreats.

During that time, there were a lot of people in our community who were coming out of the drug epidemic. Many of them ended up in our store talking to us. We loved seeing and hearing from them so much that we tried to figure out how we could help them. Our goal was to make our community healthier than they were before.

We felt that it was necessary to take the people outside of their immediate surroundings to begin their health journey. So we began hosting retreats outside of New York City to expose the attendees to a different environment; one that was peaceful, quiet and conducive to different types of healing experiences. We were an amazing couple, and the relationship eventually led to marriage. Our union lasted for 15 years, but unfortunately, we divorced, and he passed away due to a brain aneurysm.

Transitions

New York City was a great place for film and film festivals. I attended them every chance I got. I remember attending an African American Film Festival in Brooklyn, where I served as a vendor. I was in the health and nutrition business making protein shakes. It was there that I met my then future husband. This was another pivotal transition in my life. We dated and decided to get married. I fell in love with his artwork and his stories. Although he was not well known at the time, I connected him with the resources that he needed and eventually he became an accomplished and well-known artist.

Because I was connected to numerous individuals in the entertainment industry, had conducted many readings, and was married to an artist, I decided to explore the possibility of creating my own film. All my previous experiences helped to create the framework in my mind to try film production.

There was a movie called "Miss Everett's Boys," that motivated me to write my own story. My first film was titled, "Nursing Tuskegee." It told the story of Black men in Alabama who participated in an unethical medical experiment and were exploited as a result. From there, I created 37 additional films. My interest in filmmaking was born and had taken off. Making films was a life-changing transitional phase of my life. I believed that I could do anything.

I exposed my daughter to acting at an early age. She consistently performed throughout her childhood years, so I encouraged her to also start writing and she did. She also decided to add modeling to her career. After she began having children of her own, she in turn placed them into acting and modeling as well. We all experienced what it was like being a part of the entertainment industry in New York City. It was truly a family affair. My marriage lasted 15 years, but unfortunately we eventually divorced.

REFLECTIONS

What major transitions have you experienced in your life? How did they shape you into the person you have become or are becoming?

_____

_____

_____

_____

_____

_____

_____

_____

_____

_____

_____

_____

_____

_____

_____

_____

_____

_____

_____

_____

Coming Full Circle – The Joy and Pain

I constantly visited my family in Washington, D.C. My mother, sisters, and brothers all lived there. However, there was a family friend of my brother who liked me. He drove me to my prom, attended my graduation, and was an integral part of my life growing up.

Sometime after my divorce, he started contacting me and expressed an interest in me romantically. My sister informed me that he had always liked me, but I was oblivious to it. However, eventually we started dating and got married. This relationship came full circle, from childhood to marriage, then to caregiving.

We had a long-distance relationship given that he lived in D.C. and I in New York City. We would alternate cities, staying a month at a time and enjoyed experiencing various things. It felt as if we were always on a honeymoon. However, during one of my visits, he had his first stroke. This was the beginning of his decline. He had five more after that.

Shortly after the first stroke, I moved to Washington, D.C. to care for my husband. As his health began to decline further, I did everything within my power to give him a better quality of life.

At age 78, out of all of my experiences, the one common thread I see is to always stay open to finding joy in each one. The joy of having my daughter and grandchildren with me as I recovered and cared for my husband was priceless. Having my grandchildren in my presence full-time gave me a new lease on life and joy unspeakable. I had a new found opportunity to pour into them, encourage them, and push them up close and in person. As a result, my grandson has been in films since he was 3 years old.

Finding joy in caring for my husband also gave me a new purpose in life. Going on trips, cruises, and adding quality to his life did us both good. Reminiscing about my time in New York City – meeting amazing people, producing films, and hosting wellness retreats – also added joy to my life.

That said, my message to everyone out there is to find your joy. No matter what the experience, good or bad, you can find joy through it all.

REFLECTIONS

What are some things that bring you joy?

_____

_____

_____

_____

_____

_____

_____

_____

_____

_____

_____

_____

_____

_____

_____

_____

_____

_____

_____

Bio

Ruth Harris

Ruth Harris is a mom, health educator, gallery curator, and film producer. She received a master's degree in childhood education and retired from the New York Board of Education after 30 years. Although she's a native Washingtonian where she currently resides, Ruth lived in New York City for more than 50 years.

She has a daughter and five grandchildren. She enjoys the fine arts, performing arts, and spending time with family, especially her daughter Isis, and her grandchildren.

To connect with Ruth Harris:

Instagram: @ruth.harris.5268
Facebook: facebook.com/ruth.harris.5268

CHAPTER 3

POWER

BY MICHELLE BROWN

What is power? Merriam-Webster defines it as the ability to act or produce an effect. That means power enables us to act. Let's think about where it comes from.

When I think about power as it relates to energy, I wonder about its source. For example, electricity is derived from a source of power. The power source for electricity is a steam turbine that uses several types of fuel such as fossil fuel, nuclear, or solar thermal energy.

Now let's approach the concept of power in the human sense. Our power comes from a source that energizes us. Our power is enhanced by the challenges and struggles we experience. We in turn tap into that power using our inner strength, wisdom, and authority given to us by God through our experiences. When a storm hits in our lives, that becomes our weakest moment, and we gain our strength from our inner power. That inner power is fueled by a higher power or supernatural power from God. Below is a mnemonic I created using the word POWER.

P	Persever-ance
O	Ownership
W	Wisdom
E	Endurance
R	Resilience

These words represent qualities that support my inner power throughout my journey of survival, purpose, and empowerment. It took perseverance for me to survive, discover my purpose, and engage in empowerment. I had to take ownership of my doubts and fears as it related to my unwelcome medical diagnosis and not let it control me.

I gained wisdom as I recognized the signs from my body and as I questioned doctors about my diagnosis. I endured the discomfort and weakness I experienced while waiting for my new heart although there was no guarantee that I would get one. Lastly, I had to be resilient to withstand all the difficulties and challenges I experienced throughout my life despite my diagnosis.

REFLECTIONS

Now it is time to reflect on your own personal story and think about your own power. Go back and review the mnemonic I mentioned above. If you were to create your own mnemonic for your inner power, what would it be?

P	
O	
W	
E	
R	

Survival

I have had a strong will to survive since childhood. It is because my mom died at such an early age. At age 21 she lost her life due to heart failure and arrhythmia when I was three years old. That may be when my fear of death began. While my father was holding me near her casket at the funeral, I do not remember saying to my mother, "Arlene, get up." However, every time I heard family members talk about my reaction at the funeral, it felt like a movie I constantly replayed in my head over and over again. I was so young, but that memory was so vivid in my mind to this day, I don't know if it was real. Regardless, it will forever be etched in my mind as a snapshot of a memory.

The First Scar

I have often wondered if I am the one who found my mother when she died. I asked my uncle if I did and he told me that it's possible; however, he was not certain. If I did find her or even saw her body moved from our home by first responders, that would explain why I was so petrified. Her death created an emotional scar to a wound that would reopen each time I had a medical crisis.

My mother's death certainly had an impact on me. I feared that I would die at 21, too, although I hadn't experienced any heart issues, so I thought. Looking back, I wondered if I had any heart issues that had gone unnoticed?

During my early twenties, my doctor told me that the birth control pills I was taking were causing me to have high blood pressure. She said that if I did not stop taking them, they would put me six feet under. My fear of death came rushing back and I immediately stopped taking the pills. I never went back to that doctor again. I was relieved, thinking I would not develop a heart problem after all.

Childbirth and Medical Neglect

The same fear of death returned when I experienced a health crisis in April 1992. I was pregnant with my son, Miguel, and it was four days past my due date. I had been experiencing breathing issues for two weeks prior. Initially, I did not worry. I had been told during Lamaze class that breathing discomfort was normal towards the end of pregnancy. However, on this day I grew more concerned.

My husband took me to see my primary care doctor after I told him how I was feeling. After my doctor examined me he recommended that I go to the hospital to have my labor induced. My husband drove me to the hospital and when we reported to labor and delivery, we explained to the doctor that we were there to have my labor induced. He noticed that my heart was racing and mentioned that they needed to find out why. Unfortunately, he said it was the end of his shift. It appeared to me that he didn't relay that information to the next doctor who came on duty because the team proceeded to induce my labor.

While I was going through labor, I knew something was wrong. I felt so strained and tired as I pushed for the baby to be born. I thought that I might die during childbirth, but I did not tell anyone. I knew I had to hold on and be strong. I just kept praying asking God to help me to endure the birth of my child.

I believed that if I could survive delivering my baby, I could rest and recover. I did not want my child to be raised without me since I grew up without my mother. I did not want to die and leave my husband either. So, I continued to pray as I fought for my survival. God answered that prayer, and I saw my beautiful baby boy born.

After giving birth, I stayed in the hospital for a few days. I discovered that I was coughing up blood. I told the nurse, and she said it was happening as a result of screaming during childbirth. I knew that was a lie because that never happened. I also knew that screaming would not cause me to cough up blood like that.

However, no one followed up with me to determine why it was happening. I was discharged and sent home with my baby. I was not feeling well at all that night. People were entering my room to visit me and the baby. However, I could not enjoy the visit because I was so sick and exhausted.

A day after I was discharged from the hospital, I still did not feel any better. My husband took me to my HMO since that is where I had been going for my general medical care. I was there for an hour before being referred to the hospital. My husband took me back to the hospital as I was struggling to breathe. I was told that they were going to intubate me for treatment.

After intubating me and taking X-rays, the medical staff discovered that I had pneumonia. I was treated with multiple medications, including antibiotics. But I do not remember all of the names. I do know that I experienced side effects such as skin peeling. That was a small price to pay because the medical staff were doing everything in their power to help me get better.

My Diagnosis

Some days after the pneumonia cleared up, the doctors discovered that I had a heart problem. I was diagnosed with peripartum cardiomyopathy and an enlarged heart. Peripartum cardiomyopathy is a condition that some people get during pregnancy or soon after childbirth. The heart muscle stretches more than normal and becomes weak. It may cause problems, such as heart failure. This means the heart can't pump the blood your body needs properly. It can be long-term and sometimes causes death.

The doctors were still trying to learn more about my diagnosis, including what caused it to happen. I was treated with traditional heart medications that included lisinopril and blood thinners such as heparin and coumadin. I remember being in the hospital on Easter Sunday because I watched "The Ten Commandments" on television.

My stay was for at least fifteen days because the doctors wanted to be sure that they were providing me with the best treatment. They also wanted to make sure that I was going to be well enough to go home and care for my baby. While in the hospital, I asked for information to read about my condition. There was not much literature on it from what I was told. Not only did I want to educate myself about my diagnosis, but just as importantly, I wanted to learn how I was going to cope with it as well as survive with it. Because the literature was outdated, my doctor didn't want to give me information originating from a study at Cook County Hospital in Chicago, during the 1970s. However, I insisted on getting the information and it was given to me.

Upon reading it, I learned that mothers who were diagnosed with peripartum cardiomyopathy often did not live past their children's fourth birthday. The study indicated that some mothers' hearts could potentially shrink within a year. However, the ability of the heart to shrink depended on the type of heart that the mother had. The study referenced a flabby heart versus other types. In my case, the medical team did not seem to expect my heart to shrink. I was distraught, but I fought with prayer.

I eventually went home to raise my baby and recover. I continued to be fearful with thoughts that I could die at any time. But I knew that I had a baby boy to care for. I also wanted to enjoy my time with him and my husband. As I got stronger, I was told to walk two miles a day to help strengthen my heart. So, I would put my sweet baby boy in his stroller and push it as I walked those two miles each day. I spent three months at home with my baby before returning to work.

After returning to work, I realized that I had not recovered completely. I continued to see my cardiologist and primary care doctors for follow-up appointments and check-ups. Unfortunately, my cardiologist said that I had not recovered well enough to continue working. She recommended that I apply for social security disability until I was strong enough to work. This was scary for me because I knew there was no guarantee that I would recover well enough to return. Again, I knew there was a possibility that my health might not improve, and I could die.

Sometimes the thought of me dying was suffocating and I did not want to talk about it. In my eyes, death was not an option. I was afraid of what could happen to me as it relates to heart failure, especially since my mother died from it. I asked my primary care doctor many "what if" questions and she would tell me not to look for red herrings. It was like I was waiting for the other shoe to drop. I could not live freely because my mind was consumed with thoughts of my heart issues threatening my life. I was in survival mode and on high alert for more than 20 years.

Pregnant Again

My husband and I moved to North Carolina in 1993 after I filed for Social Security disability benefits because we could no longer afford to live in Maryland. He took a job at a family member's auto repair shop. While in North Carolina, I discovered that I was pregnant a second time. Our son was about a year old. I missed my period and that was a clear indication that I was pregnant.

I took an at-home pregnancy test which also indicated I was pregnant. I was receiving medical care for my heart problem at the University of North Carolina (UNC) Hospital in Chapel Hill at the time. I called the nurse in the cardiac clinic and told her that I was pregnant. She told me to go to my local clinic and have a blood pregnancy test done. I had the test done and the results confirmed what I knew to be true.

I called the nurse back to let her know that my pregnancy was confirmed with the blood test. At that time, she told me that I could not have the baby and that she was going to schedule an appointment for me to have an abortion procedure. I asked if it was possible for me to have the baby and she said that if I carried the baby, I may not be able to make it to full-term based on the condition of my heart at the time. She indicated that I and/or my baby could die.

I was concerned about having an abortion because of my religious background. Was I making the right decision or would God disapprove of me aborting my child? Some of my family members were part of the Pentecostal Church and Church of God in Christ. I worried that they would not approve or judge me. I thought they would not support me in my decision because they believed abortions were wrong. However, to my surprise, my family members supported me by saying, "You do what you have to do." That dispelled my fear of disapproval.

I had the abortion procedure when I was six weeks pregnant. My heart had weakened significantly just after carrying our second baby for that short amount of time. I had to return to the hospital to stay for some days to get medical treatment. I was given dopamine and other drugs to strengthen my heart, but my ejection fraction was low, which measures the heart's ability to pump oxygen-rich blood out to the body. In a healthy heart, the fraction is a higher number. A low number means that the heart has difficulty keeping up with your body's needs.

The Cardiac Study

Yet again, there was a conversation about how weak my heart had gotten and what to do about it. It was recommended that my name get placed on the heart transplant list. After taking several vaccinations, tests, examinations, and/or procedures I was placed on the list. During that time, I was given the opportunity to participate in a cardiac study. I was told that I could join the study to test a new cardiac drug if I was interested. I agreed to participate. They made no promises, but there was the possibility that I might not need a heart transplant if my heart improved as a result of the study.

It was a blind study which meant I would not know if I would be taking the actual drug or the placebo. I would not find out that information until after the study was completed and received a stipend for participating. I had nothing to lose because I was on the heart transplant list. If the study

43

helped me, my name would be moved to the inactive list. Subsequently, I would be removed from the list altogether.

I participated in the study between 1993 and 1994. Initially, I traveled to UNC Chapel Hill once a week. My part in the study included me taking the medication provided at home. Then I had to report to the hospital for a visit with the cardiac nurse. She checked my blood pressure, oxygen level, and temperature. Then we walked up and down the hallway to see how well I responded. After our walk, she checked my vitals again. Lastly, I received my next dose of medication and my stipend.

We moved back to Maryland in 1994. My husband continued to drive me back and forth from Maryland to North Carolina to participate in the study. After I completed it, it was revealed that I had in fact been taking the actual drug they were studying. The drug, Carvedilol (Coreg), improved my heart function.

Carvedilol is used alone or together with other medicines to treat high blood pressure (hypertension); to prevent congestive heart failure; or to treat left ventricular dysfunction. My case number as a Carvedilol study participant was included in the *New England Journal of Medicine* from what I was told.

Participating in the study gave me a new lease on life since my heart function was significantly improved. While I still experienced fear, I had a break from experiencing any medical crises. I was able to go back to college and complete my bachelor's degree in accounting while on disability. My cardiologist approved me to go back to work, and I was no longer considered disabled. In 1999, I started my first job out of college as an auditor for one of the top minority-owned CPA firms in the world.

The Second Scar

I didn't have another medical crisis until the year 2000. The stress from my employment with the CPA firm was primarily the cause of it. My heart got weak again and I had to be hospitalized for treatment. I was also tested to see if I would benefit from a defibrillator. The results determined that I was indeed a candidate for one, and it was implanted during that week. I received my first physical scar for a heart-related surgical procedure. However, it represented the second scar in my journey.

A few days after the defibrillator was implanted, I received the shock of my life, literally. The nurse put me in the bathroom to take a shower and thought I was strong enough to do so by myself. I started showering and at some point, the defibrillator shocked me and would not stop. I screamed at the top of my lungs. Of course, nurses started running down the hall to get to me. They put me on a stretcher and worked to calm me down. I was so frightened and thought I was going to die. I said, "Father God in the name of Jesus," and one of the nurses replied, "Yes, call on Him."

I eventually calmed down as I continued to pray. Clearly it was too soon for me to shower on my own. I needed to regain my strength. I made sure to tell the medical staff to continue to have someone to assist me when it was time for me to wash up, rather than have me do it alone. I was eventually discharged some days later. I was afraid to shower at home for a while. For a while, I relied on washing up in the sink with my husband nearby. I had a break from going through medical crises for several years.

Reopening the Scar

However, in February 2014, I had another medical scare. I went to the doctor to get my defibrillator checked. During my visit, he mentioned that he wanted to schedule me for a procedure at the hospital to replace it with a new one that had more capability. He looked at my records and discovered that the wires had not been replaced since the early 2000's. He also looked at the video from the camera and saw that the wires were wound up. This was a complication he did not expect.

He also shared with me that performing the procedure at the hospital with the right set up would be to my benefit in case he had to perform open heart surgery on me. You see, he needed to cut out the old wires and replace them with new ones when he implanted the new defibrillator. He told me that there would be 1/1000th of a chance that he could cut me when removing the wires. He said if he did cut me, he would have to perform open heart surgery. That frightened me because I had never had any surgeries on my heart. I had prayed for God to heal my heart, and I honestly thought I would not need surgery. I was also afraid that surgery, if required, could be unsuccessful, and cause me to die.

I understood that the doctor needed to reopen my scar to insert the new defibrillator. However, my fear intensified with the revelation of a possible surgical complication. This in turn opened up the wound tied to my lifelong emotional scar. I was worried from that day forward. Still, I knew that I needed to rely on my faith and in order to have peace. I prayed and started writing a song to cope. I told God that I would finish it after I got out of the hospital.

The procedure was successful. In fact, an anesthesiologist visited me in recovery. He said, " the doctor cut and cut, but he did not cut you." I did not require open heart surgery, and I went home the next day. I finished writing the song after I recovered. I recorded my song "Who Knew" in the studio and released it to digital platforms in 2016.

As time passed and I recognized that I was surviving, my fear decreased. I was doing everything that healthy people could do and lead a normal life. I worked out 5 or 6 days a week. I worked full-time. I completed college degrees. I sang in the choir. And while I had my health challenges, no one knew it unless I told them. Not only was I surviving, but I was living. I could finally just live, stop worrying, and trust God.

The Latest Scar – My Journey to Healing

In 2022, I started having issues with my heart again. I was hospitalized twice that year. I was told that my heart was weak and that I needed a transplant. While the doctor did not tell me I was dying, I knew I was in serious condition. I was told that I could not go home during that second hospital stay. My fear was paralyzing then, and I could not rest.

The chaplain visited me a few days out of the week. Although she would pray with me, sometimes I was still not at ease. One day she taught me this stretching exercise and asked me to stretch my foot to touch the foot-board of the bed. She asked, "Can you feel your feet?" I said, "Yes," and surprisingly it seemed to calm me down. She told me to repeat it whenever I felt anxious.

I also had anxiety from hearing the dings and alarms on the machines in the hospital, whether it was from my room or another patient's room. I feared that my heart could be in major trouble each time I heard those sounds. However, I realized during that time that I had to trust the process, the medical staff, and certainly God. I coped by doing things to take my mind off what I was going through such as praying, writing, playing solitaire, candy crush, watching television, singing, and exercising my arms and legs while I waited for my heart.

There was a tremendous amount of psychological impact on me through-out my journey. Starting with my mother's death from heart failure, I developed anxiety because I feared that my fate would be the same as my mom. When I was diagnosed with heart failure my anxiety increased. However, I had to pray, rely on my faith, learn to trust the process, talk about my concerns, and just live. I needed to focus on what I could control and not let my anxiety control or paralyze me.

As I reflect on the impact that my mother's death has had on my life, I think about the scars that remained. Over the years, I did not think about the scars. I just continued to operate in survival mode. I now realize that my mom's death left me with invisible mental and emotional scars which ran far deeper than my physical ones. My physical scars healed. However, the mental and emotional scars continued to be fed by the loss of my mom; the fear of losing my own life; and the fear of losing another loved one.

REFLECTIONS

Have you discovered any mental or emotional scars that may have impacted your life?

_____

_____

_____

_____

_____

_____

_____

_____

_____

_____

_____

_____

_____

_____

_____

_____

_____

_____

_____

_____

_____

Purpose

Merriam-Webster defines purpose as something set up as an object or end to be attained. It also references the words intention, resolution, and determination. When I think of my purpose, I never truly expounded on what that meant to me or for my life.

I have heard others say to a person that he or she may have a calling on his or her life. However, as I reflect on my journey, I can say that my experiences represent my personal calling with intention, resolution, and determination. In 2020, I began to reminisce about the calling on my life and wrote a song about it. There was a tugging in my spirit, but I was not sure of the calling, the purpose, or the intention. Following are lyrics from my song, "A Calling On My Life."

God has a calling on my life that I cannot seem to shake,

He has a calling on my life that I know I can't forsake,

When the enemy comes my way, I take my focus away,

But God has a calling, a calling,

God has a calling on my life.

I have found purpose in my journey, struggles, and challenges. A portion of my purpose is to stand firm, move forward, and tell my story of hope and resilience to as many people as possible. I also know that it is my responsibility to share my knowledge about what I have learned from my experience. Throughout my journey I have learned the following things which have helped me to cope:

• Acknowledging my fears and talking about it.

• Seeking help and support from others including therapists.

• Looking for the positive aspects and engaging in simple activities that bring about personal joy.

• Writing down my feelings and experiences.

• Telling my story to others and listening to others.

• Advocating for myself.

REFLECTIONS

I shared my song lyrics about the calling on my life. Do you have a yearning or feel like there is a calling on your life?

_____

_____

_____

_____

_____

_____

_____

_____

_____

_____

_____

_____

_____

_____

_____

_____

_____

_____

Empowerment

When I think of empowerment, I see it as enlightenment that brings about the freedom to step into one's own power after going through a major storm, struggle, journey, or challenge. I experienced emotional, psychological, and physical challenges throughout my journey to my healing. As I previously shared, my emotional and psychological challenges began in my childhood as I grieved the death of my mom. I may have been in denial or in disbelief. I attribute that to what my relatives told me about my reaction when I viewed my mom's body. I appeared to have rejected that she was dead because I told her to get up at her funeral as I cried. I reacted as if I thought she was just merely sleeping and ignoring my request. I was truly too young to understand the concept of death and grief. And consequently, it led to my anxiety and fear of death which carried on into my adulthood.

When I was diagnosed with heart failure in 1992, I was reminded that my mother died of heart failure as well. That fear of death resurfaced and came rushing back with a feeling of suffocation and powerlessness. However, I wanted and needed to survive for the sake of my husband, my son, as well as myself. I also knew that there were many things I wanted to accomplish for myself and those who came before me. So, I fought with everything in me by gathering information and learning what I needed to do to maintain my survival.

My 30-year journey from heart failure to healing by way of a heart transplant enabled me to walk in my truth toward self-empowerment. However, it was not an easy process in my effort to gain confidence, control, and authority over my life. And while I had my faith to rely on, I still had doubt. I remember hearing other Christians say God has not given us a spirit of fear and that we should not be fearful. Hearing this sometimes made me feel guilty or condemned because I am a woman of faith.

I mentioned that concern to the chaplain when I was in the hospital waiting for my new heart. She reminded me that it was alright to be afraid. She also said that we should acknowledge to God that we are afraid and draw closer to Him instead of holding on to the fear. Then she referenced the Bible verse that says, "Immediately the father of the child cried out and said with tears, "Lord, I believe; help my unbelief!" (Mark 9:24 New King James Version) I repeated that verse multiple times when I began to have doubts. Hearing that verse and letting it sink into my thoughts worked to liberate me in a sense. It allowed me to express freedom from the guilt of feeling so afraid.

My steps toward self-empowerment did not consist of a set standard. However, as I acknowledge a specific fear or concern that may hold me captive, I work to release it from my mind, body, soul, and spirit. In turn, this allows me to move in the right direction towards achieving inner peace. Each time I stand in my truth, own it, and let go of any associated pain or guilt, I regain just a little bit more of my power inch by inch. I understand that I must be patient to allow myself grace. Some suggestions that I recommend for working towards self-empowerment are as follows:

- Observing your own mental and emotional processes.

- Engaging in self-care.

- Seeking out ways to motivate yourself.

- Giving yourself grace.

- Finding an accountability partner or support group.

- Standing in your truth, acknowledging your fears, and releasing them to achieve inner peace.

REFLECTIONS

What enables you to walk in your truth toward self-empowerment?

_____

_____

_____

_____

_____

_____

_____

_____

_____

_____

_____

_____

_____

_____

_____

_____

_____

_____

_____

_____

Bio
Michelle M. Brown

Michelle Brown is originally from Bunnlevel, NC, and currently resides in Temple Hills, MD. She is a wife of 37 years and a mother to a 33-year-old son. In 2021, she wrote and self-published her book, *My Life Isn't Perfect, But My Testimony Is...I Don't Look Like What I Have Been Through* which garnered her an International Impact Book Award in March of 2024.

Michelle received a bachelor's degree in accounting from the University of the District of Columbia; a master's degree in accounting and finance from the University of Maryland University College; and a master's degree in cost estimating from the Naval Postgraduate School.

To connect with Michelle:
Email Address: MichelleB.Gospel@gmail.com
Instagram: @MichelleBGospel
Facebook: http://facebook.com/MichelleBGospel

CHAPTER 4

I SEE YOU

BY DR. FLORENCE CHAMPAGNE

"You have a scar," she said to me as she pointed at my chest. The little girl must have been 5 or 6 years old. She was my co-worker's daughter who accompanied her to the office for the day. The scar she was referring to was from the incision that went straight down the middle of my chest during my open-heart surgery. It was my sternum, to be exact.

While I appreciated her raw, inquisitive spirit and frankness in pointing it out to me, I wondered what would happen next? Should I tell her that I had open heart surgery; or, that I had coronary artery disease or blocked arteries? Would she even understand? Do I dare go into exactly what happened? I was stumped in the face of a young child, not knowing exactly how to respond properly. It's as if she was saying, "I see you." Even though I don't look view my scar as an attemtion grabber, I was more impressed that she even noticed and acknowledged her.

"Yes, I have a scar," I replied. "But why?" she asked. I should have expected her to ask. "The doctor had to fix my heart," I said. "But why?" she asked again. Here we go. Do I tell her that I had 99% blockage in my Left Anterior Descending (LAD) artery, also known as the widow maker? Do I tell her about the bypass? Do I tell her about coronary artery disease? Thank God her mother came.

"She has a scar," she said to her mother as she pointed at me. I told mom how impressed I was. That was my first experience where I used my words to summarize not only what happened, but the fact that people may want to know, even a child. I felt that whether I am ready or not, I will have to provide an explanation.

The Cover Up

I had on a blouse that revealed my scar. My "heart" sister, (another sister who had open heart surgery), saw my chest one day and said to me,

"You show your scar?" Her tone made me feel as if I had done something wrong as she looked at it.

I thought highly of her and her status. For a moment I second-guessed myself, wondering if I should conform to how she felt. The larger issue was that I was confronted by someone who thought I should cover myself to make them, or others feel comfortable. I said further, "No, I don't cover up my scar, as a matter of fact, I don't think about covering or hiding it. I am proud of what God has brought me through."

REFLECTIONS

Have you ever felt there was something you either needed to cover up or change about yourself to conform? If so, how did it make you feel and how did you respond?

_____

_____

_____

_____

_____

_____

_____

_____

_____

_____

_____

_____

_____

_____

_____

_____

_____

_____

_____

From Pain to Purpose

Have you ever felt like this is the end? Have you ever wanted to just break down or give up? On my road to recovery, I secretly wanted to give up. No one knew what was going on deep down inside. I was struggling just to breathe. It hurt just to move, or go to the bathroom, I looked like a mess. I was uninsured, unemployed, and felt as though I didn't have anything to live for. The reality of my situation hit me like a ton of bricks. I felt hopeless. I recalled thinking that I just wanted to curse God and die. I was depressed.

Leading up to my heart attack, I felt that from the emergency room and doctor's visits to the various tests I had to take, no one was listening to me, or even cared. At every turn, I was being rejected, misdiagnosed, and dismissed by physicians and hospitals. I was experiencing shortness of breath, and various other symptoms, such as a sensation in my jaw and lower back pain. Most of the time, I could not even describe or articulate what I was going through.

After approximately a year of going back and forth to the hospital, I did not even want to go back anymore. During the last visit, the ER doctor recommended that I seek therapy, as if the pain were all in my head. I walked away vowing to never go back to the hospital again.

As time went on, I met a cardiologist. For the first time, I felt as though someone was listening to me as I described what I had been going through. Baffled from all my hospital visits and tests, he looked at me and said, "Let me ask you something; what kind of insurance do you have?" I replied, "I don't have any." He let me know that was the real reason why I did not receive certain diagnostic tests to see what was going on with my heart.

He planned for me to have a cardiac catheterization, which revealed 99.9% blockage in my Left Anterior Descending artery. By the time they were rolling me into the operating room, the only thing I heard them say was, "If we don't hurry up and perform emergency open heart surgery, we're going to lose you." There was also a 50% chance of that happening regardless. The only thing I could think of at that moment was that I didn't finish my book. I thought that I was about to die without completing the one thing God told me to do, which was to tell my story.

Surviving was mixed with gratitude and depression. Feeling the wound on my chest was too much to bear, which led to psychological pain and scars.

It was as if someone had violated me by cutting my chest open. I cried every day for a while. I did not know what I had done wrong in order to deserve this. No one would listen to me. Then I began to suffer. As I was crying in my bed of affliction, having internal conversations, in my deepest, darkest hour, I asked *"Why did you save me?"* I could hear the words *"So you can tell your story."*

REFLECTIONS

Have you ever wanted to give up? How did you overcome some of the challenges, barriers, and inner struggles to go on to become more resilient and empowered?

_____

_____

_____

_____

_____

_____

_____

_____

_____

_____

_____

_____

_____

_____

_____

_____

_____

_____

_____

_____

The Sign

Later that year, and as I continued to recover from my open-heart surgery, I went for a job interview. Someone sent me a job announcement and told me to quickly reply because it was about to close. Prior to that, I recall going for a walk, praying that I'd get the job. It was in God's hands now, but I really wanted it.

I prayed and I walked; I walked, and I prayed. There's something about the solitude and sacredness of walking and talking to God. The next thing I knew, I was called in for an interview. Near the end of it, the supervisor told me that she had interviewed several candidates and was close to making a decision until I came along.

She shared with me that she had prayed for a sign from God, to know that she was hiring the right person for the job. Although I was highly qualified for it with all of the right credentials, when I walked into the office, and she saw the scar on my chest, she said that she knew that was the sign that she asked for. My scar was a clear sign, imagine that. Her husband had open heart surgery, and she was his caregiver, so she knew exactly what it was, and she knew that I was the one for the job. This was an interview like no other. We both became emotional.

"The 4th Quarter"

I recently heard someone say, "The win doesn't happen until the 4th quarter." At age 66, I began to look at my life differently. Metaphorically, the 4th quarter refers to the later stages of life. Although the age range may vary, it typically refers to age 60 to79. It's a time to reflect on our lives, pursue new passions and focus on our legacy and purpose.

The year was 2012 when I nearly lost my life. This near-death experience made me fearless! I was living out loud, enjoying my life, and pursuing my goals. Surviving a heart attack followed by open-heart surgery gave me a different perspective. God wanted me here for a reason! I felt like I needed to run and do all that God told me to do because tomorrow was not promised. I was in the 4th quarter.

It was liberating to know that I didn't have to worry about things that didn't matter. I had a vision of going before the Lord and Him asking me, "What did you do with the gifts and talents that I gave you?" As I laid on my recovery bed, I felt a sense of urgency. I pulled out my laptop and finished my first book called *Inez's Granddaughter*. Having experienced inequities in the healthcare system and trying to fight for my life, I put on my social worker hat and became an advocate, not only for myself but for others.

Today I am a two-time Amazon bestselling author, an artist and a health advocate. God gave me purpose through my pain. Someone once told me that I was a "late bloomer." I shrugged it off but began to question their comment later in life especially when every day seemed like a constant struggle. I couldn't figure out why things weren't working out for me. However, that comment took on a deeper meaning and I wanted to know more. I began hearing it again and other phrases like "the 4th quarter," repeatedly from different people, sometimes years apart. I have often heard spiritual and/or religious people say, "The Lord told me to tell you…" I believe that when you get a message from God, you will receive confirmation soon after in various ways. This was my confirmation.

It was almost 1989. I needed to break free. I needed to breathe and expand my mind; I needed more air. I also needed to think differently and be around people who did also. I didn't know it then but not only was I becoming an adult at an early age , but I was also becoming more mature in my thinking. So I decided to move and even began changing my thought processes. I was in my 30's and in the 2nd quarter of my life.

Fast forward to Quarter 3, at age 53, it took me nearly losing my life to start living my life. The lesson – don't wait until you think you are at the end of your life to start living, thinking that something might happen, or that you're not enough.

As early as age 4, I recall helping my great aunt, who was also my babysitter. She was obese, limited in her mobility, and had all sorts of other medical issues. I had to become her eyes, arms and legs, running up and down the steps getting things for her throughout the day. I didn't know it then, but I became a caregiver at a very young age, bathing her, helping her get dressed, brushing her hair, and even emptying her slop bucket. I was her little helper and was proud of it! These early childhood experiences impacted me and influenced my decision to become a social worker. I felt the need to not only care for the elderly, but to fight for injustices regarding healthcare. Such a burden to help others comes with a cost.

REFLECTIONS

What are some of your childhood experiences that helped you shape the decisions you have made or are making as an adult?

_____

_____

_____

_____

_____

_____

_____

_____

_____

_____

_____

_____

_____

_____

_____

_____

_____

_____

_____

_____

_____

"The Superwoman Syndrome"

Having a burden and passion to help others can be both a blessing and a curse. My grandmother had a saying, "right don't wrong nobody." At the time, I just thought she was using bad English. But later in life I found myself reflecting on some of her old sayings and others by my ancestors, even though I thought some of them didn't make any sense. I often reflect on the past, just like the Sankofa bird, a symbol from the people of Ghana, representing the importance of learning from the past to build a successful future.

There have been several liberating moments leading up to publishing this book anthology that have confirmed that I'm doing exactly what I was called to do. I have either been fired from jobs or rolled out of buildings on a stretcher. I could feel the stress and pain of it all over the years. I was working 10-to-14-hour days. No matter how hard I worked, it seemed I was always behind. As a social worker, I was always overloaded with more clients than I had time for. But there was a specific time when I was rolled out on a stretcher, that I knew that I could not go back. I could not face that level of pain again.

Understanding and accepting that stress could kill me, I had to make some major personal changes. I could no longer be "superwoman" to every-one. If I chose to pick up that mantle again, it would be the end of me. I learned some time ago that I was a "people pleaser." I wanted everything to be right with the world and did whatever it took to try and make it so. What a burden to carry!

After God saved me, I had renewed faith and God's grace showed me that He was in control and would take care of me. I began to feel fearless! Although I was still lacking medical coverage and was not sure how I was going to pay my bills, I felt like I was eating manna from Heaven. God truly provided. My bills were being paid from sources that I can't even name. I knew that He was carrying me through when I couldn't carry my-self. I was also confident that He had not brought me this far just to leave me. He has shown me time and time again that He is with me. Why would I doubt Him ever again?

If I am challenged or something tries to bring me down, I think about how I couldn't breathe, had no money, almost lost my life, and how God car-ried me through every situation.

REFLECTIONS

Name a time when you had to change your perspective and set boundaries and limits. What was the outcome?

_____

_____

_____

_____

_____

_____

_____

_____

_____

_____

_____

_____

_____

_____

_____

_____

_____

_____

Bio

Dr. Florence Champagne

Dr. Florence Champagne is a patient advocate, consultant, strategist and multiple bestselling author. She earned a Bachelor of Arts degree in Art Therapy from George Mason University and a master's in social work from Howard University, respectively.

She is the CEO and Founder of the Open My Heart Foundation, Inc., a 501c3 non-profit organization. Her advocacy work includes initiating two pieces of key legislation, "Maryland Medical Assistance" (HB666) and "Health Insurance Required Coverage for Calcium Score Testing" (SB60), a screening for early detection of heart disease to prevent heart attacks. Both bills passed the House and Senate, impacting more than 6 million Marylanders.

Dr. Champagne is highly regarded as a thought leader and is often sought after by organizations to speak. Originally from Philadelphia, Penn., she currently resides in Upper Marlboro, Maryland. She is the devoted mother of one son.

To connect with Dr. Champagne:

Email: Fchampagne@openmyheartfoundation.org
Facebook: www.facebook.com/florence.d.champagne
Instagram: @champagne_florence
LinkedIn: dr-florence-champagne-086337243
Cell: 240-389-4361

CHAPTER 5

RESTORATION: RECLAIMING MY LIFE AFTER THE STROKE

BY ELENA CRUSOE AIKEN

I read somewhere that storytelling is the process of using facts and narrative to communicate something to your audience. That is a good description of what's to follow, but it does not tell the whole story of who I am. However, because I do believe in the power of a good story, I decided to be a part of this anthology and share mine with you. It's filled with twists and turns and ups and downs, but most importantly, it's also filled with a sense of hope. Unlike the physical scars that my fellow authors talked about in their chapters, my scars can't be seen by the naked eye because they are internal and were formed as a result of the various trials and tribulations I endured. Nonetheless, they played an integral part in my will to survive and overcome. As you continue reading, it is my desire to encourage you to see beyond the roadblocks and limitations that you will face along life's journey despite the scars that will form as a result.

My Humble Roots

I grew up in poverty in rural South Carolina in the 50s and 60s, one of eleven children from a sharecropper father who abandoned us and my mother when I was just a little girl. There is not much to say about him because he was never around much and by the time he left for good he left my mother with a whole lot of mouths to feed. However, I forgave him near the end of his life and visited him nearly every day in the hospital before he died.

My mother was a kind, creative, and gracious woman, often displaying humility in her interactions with others. She exhibited a sense of style that many of her friends envied. Mom made her own clothes, as she did for her children. She also made clothing for other women who had need of an outfit for some special occasion. She also canned food from her garden so that we (and some of our neighbors) would not starve during the winter months.

With seven girls at home, she made sure our house was as immaculate as if we had a cleaning lady who showed up on a weekly basis. Not only was Mom domestically inclined, but she also believed that our home should look like those featured in *Country Living Magazine*. Most of the time it did.

Personally speaking, my personality is much like my mother's, and I also inherited her creative genes. For example, I learned how to sew as she did. I watched her make things, whether she was creating a garment or curtains for the windows. She believed, as I do, that creativity is finding new ideas or solutions to problems. She would say to me, "Use your imagination." And I would say, "Yes, mom!"

Mom grew up in Orangeburg, South Carolina, which encompasses the low country region, including the Sea Islands, designated as the Gullah Geechee cultural heritage corridor. Being a Gullah woman, food was a big deal to her, especially rice and sweet potatoes, my favorite. Frequently on our table was squash, okra, field peas, corn, and stewed tomatoes – all the veggies she planted in her garden.

REFLECTIONS

How has the experiences from your past upbringing helped to shape and mold your thinking today?

_____

_____

_____

_____

_____

_____

_____

_____

_____

_____

_____

_____

_____

_____

_____

_____

_____

_____

_____

_____

The Long Road Back: A Survivor's Story

It was Saturday morning, June 2, 2008. It was a day like no other. Not only was it my birthday, but it was also the 15th Anniversary of my company, the Elena Design Studio. I had planned a party and a jewelry shopping spree for all of my loyal customers. Suddenly, I felt weak and off balance; my vision was gone, and I could not speak. However, I thank God that my husband was at home helping me prepare for the party. Usually he would have been out doing his thing by then.

Somehow, I knew I was having a stroke and needed immediate medical attention. However, what I did not know was that I would spend the next six weeks in the hospital, recovering and enduring years of painful and difficult rehabilitation. But oddly enough, throughout this experience, I felt at peace, knowing that God loved and cared for me.

The ambulance was there in short order. The paramedics rushed upstairs with lifesaving equipment, gave me an injection of some kind of medication in my arm, and we were off to the hospital. While we were enroute, I felt a bit irritated by the impromptu disruption of my day. I did not want to believe what was happening to me. I was in denial. Afterall, I had a jewelry show to execute and customers waiting to be "wowed!" But the reality of my situation was that I was having a stroke!

From those first moments in the hospital, to weeks later in physical therapy, and even later when I was finally back home, my husband Bill supported and cared for me. The Spirit of God was always there too, encouraging me to keep my eyes on Him and not on my situation. To this day, He continues to carry me in spite of my mobility limitations.

REFLECTIONS

Have you ever had a very important event derailed because of a health issue? If so, how did you handle it?

_____

_____

_____

_____

_____

_____

_____

_____

_____

_____

_____

_____

_____

_____

_____

_____

_____

_____

_____

_____

_____

The Diagnosis: Understanding Stroke

My diagnosis was called an "ischemic," or left-brain stroke. When some-one suffers a stroke it becomes problematic for the blood vessels to carry oxygen to the cells of the brain. Consequently, brain cells become trauma-tized, and some of them die. Because every brain is unique in its neurolog-ical wiring, each of us is unique in our ability to recover from trauma.

The stroke left me unable to use the dominant side of my body effectively, which was my right side. My muscles were so weak, my fingers naturally closed as if I wanted to make a fist and my arm would hang close to my body. I also developed what is known as drop foot, where a person looks like they are dragging their foot, or they push it out because they have a hard time lifting it in order to walk normally. Those were the only two visible "scars" that indicated that I had suffered a stroke.

However, the left side of the brain (left hemisphere) is the home of our ego center. It provides us with the facts of our life, for example, our name, credentials, and where we live. People who have damage to the left hemi-sphere of the brain often lose the ability to speak because the cells in their language center have been injured. They often become geniuses at being able to determine if someone is telling the truth, thanks to the cells in their right hemisphere. Having a stroke makes it extremely difficult to live in reality.

After the doctors had done all they could do for me, and I had gone through the early stages of an extremely painful rehabilitation to stretch and retrain my muscles, I realized that becoming fully functional again would be no easy feat. Six weeks after that is when I began to slowly recover.

Although the traumatic incident left me unable to use my right side effec-tively, I began to incorporate jewelry design into my rehabilitation and physical therapy by using my left hand to create award-winning jewel-ry. The rehab technicians were very impressed at the idea that a stroke pa-tient would even attempt such a thing. Of course, I explained to them that the more I worked at it, the easier the task became. Training my left hand to become dominant was necessary. The alternative was not an option when I continued hearing my mother say, "Use your imagination."

Sadly though, my road to recovery was too arduous for me to keep my successful jewelry business open full-time. On August 10, 2008, I had to close my studio. However, my loyal clients helped to sustain me for more than a year after closing day. My community of friends, collectors, students, celebrities and customers rallied around and supported me, buying up the majority of my inventory in one day.

Initially, I thought my life as a jewelry artist was over. In August, after the stroke diagnosis, family and friends planned and executed the closing of my studio. However, they continued selling the remaining inventory. They also were able to get the word out about my illness, packed up the remainder of my belongings, and made sure the space was left clean and orderly. And through it all, they overwhelmed me with encouragement, insisting that my story was not over – instead, it was "TO BE CONTINUED."

REFLECTIONS

Can you think of a time when you thought your life was over, but later realized it was to be continued?

_____

_____

_____

_____

_____

_____

_____

_____

_____

_____

_____

_____

_____

_____

_____

_____

_____

_____

_____

The Desires of My Heart

A bride-to-be reached out to me, insisting that only I could make the jewelry for her wedding; I couldn't say no! I felt encouraged and empowered by the confidence she had in me. To my surprise, I completed her wedding jewelry and was inspired to continue to strengthen my left hand so that I could create again.

But again and again, I resigned myself to giving up on my passion – working with gemstones to design amazing jewelry and living a wonderful creative life. I had convinced myself that my remarkable and glorious creative life was gone. So I thought! Paralysis had rendered me useless for the most part. Too often, I just sat at home daydreaming. Realistically speaking, however, the ability to dream may have been my salvation. Then one day through the fog of my frustration and struggle against defeat, I heard God say to me sternly, "I GAVE YOU TWO HANDS!"

After two years in stroke recovery, I was ready to drive again, then my car died. But low and behold, a friend gave me her car – a white Mercedes! However, after years of pushing through therapy, my right hand began getting stronger and continues to do so. I have also regained my ability to walk and to drive again. So, look out world! I soon discovered that my creative talent survived unscathed. My gift resurfaced almost on its own accord, compelling me to continue designing.

Undaunted by the continuing challenges from the stroke and buoyed by a devoted following, I slowly began to produce jewelry for local boutiques and teaching workshops to new student artists. Even though this was very satisfying and I was very grateful for my blessings, my ultimate desire was to open another studio someday.

The Power of Perseverance

I have learned through this experience that perseverance really matters. It's a decision. You must look at your circumstances and ask yourself, "Is this for me?" "Am I just going to accept what has happened?" "Or am I going to work toward my dream and see what happens?" That's how the long walk back to designing again all started – in my own studio!

So, what makes me a survivor who thrives? Well, there is more than one answer to that question. I believe that if a person hasn't tried a thing, they have not earned the right to say the word "can't." What they don't realize is that their brain cells may have gone to take a rest, but those cells aren't doing anything. But I am of a different mindset. My response is, "No way, I am going to do this!" Sometimes you have to be your own cheer-leader and encourage yourself! I often try doing things before realizing I can do them. Functioning creatively again was everything to me. The more I do, the more I can do. It's a mystery. It's a part of who I am and with determination in my spirit, creativity lives within me. I am the catalyst by which it must come forth.

At the end of the fourth year after the stroke diagnosis, God spoke to me in a dream and showed me my new design studio. In the dream I was paint-ing the walls with my right hand no less. A few days later, I drove down Spring Street, and BAM!, there it was, a "For Rent" sign on unit 1107A.

I had noticed the building many times before, thinking, "I love this space; I wish this was my design studio." But in my mind I thought, what an impossibility! I told myself, "Continue driving, you have no money." But then my spirit said, "STOP." I called the phone number on the sign and was invited to look inside. There before me was the image I saw in my dream. The address, the lights overhead, the windows – I told the space manager, "It's perfect, I want it." They asked me to obtain an occupancy permit from the zoning office. But I was told that because I had a retail business it would not meet the zoning criteria for the space – BUT GOD!

I dared to dream that the "Elena Design Studio" was a possibility again – that's what dominated my thoughts and beliefs. My heart's desire became my reality. Getting the space ready was no small task. It was a struggle to obtain the occupancy permit from the zoning office. They fought me at every turn. But boy, did I prove them wrong. God had my back, yet again. Five months later, after being ignored by county authorities and jumping through multiple hoops, I obtained the zoning permit with no restrictions. Why? Because it was God's will for me and for His glory. We held the grand opening on August 10, 2012. (Ironically, that date was five years to the day after the old studio had closed.) Finally, I was back in business.

Since having a stroke, I have learned many things about how the brain works. For example, making bad choices and everyday missteps can harm your cognition. A bad diet and becoming a couch potato aren't good for the brain either, just to name a few. Given everything that I learned, I cre-ated what I call the "Healthy Brain Diet." It includes:

Avoiding sugary beverages: Consuming sugary drinks may lead to spiking blood sugar and an exaggerated insulin response. This may also trigger chronic inflammation in the brain. A far better option is to eat fresh fruit, as opposed to juices with lots of sugar added.

Stopping unhealthy sleep habits: Quality sleep is crucial for a sharp and productive mind. Consistency is key. Go to bed at the same time each night. Studies have shown that adults who sleep fewer than six hours per night may be twice as likely to have a stroke or heart attack. A change in time zone, chronic stress, and too much caffeine or alcohol can all throw off your rhythm. Abnormalities in oxygen level can be damaging to nerve cells, which may accelerate over time and contribute to memory and cognitive decline.

Moving your body: Sitting for an extended period is not healthy. This increases the risk of deep vein thrombosis, or blood clots. Make it a habit of getting up at least every hour or so to take a short walk. Exercise is very important for your overall health and more specifically, for stroke victims.

Having good dental hygiene: Practice good dental hygiene, including flossing daily. If you put yourself at risk for gum disease, you may also be increasing your chances of developing heart disease or having a stroke. Bacteria from the mouth can enter the bloodstream and result in a protein that can cause inflammation in the blood vessels.

Knowing your numbers : The target blood pressure for adults is 120/80. Blood pressure measures the force of blood against the arteries when the heart beats and rests. It is important to know your blood pressure because having hypertension increases your risk of having a stroke. It can also put a strain on your heart and kidneys.

Having a sense of purpose: If you feel that you lack a sense of purpose, do your brain a huge favor by embracing a new hobby or a do-it-yourself project and have a good attitude while doing them. Explore a passion project, volunteer, or travel. Having a reason to get up in the morning, knowing that people are depending on you, and feeling that you are making important contributions to society all help with making you feel valued and purposeful.

Focusing on the positive: Negativity is a useless emotion. Surround yourself with positive, optimistic, and like-minded people who will support you, speak the truth to you in love, and help you reach your goals. Also, think positive thoughts and speak positive affirmations over your life and believe them. You may not be where you want to be but think about how far you've come! You can change your level of joy by simply learning to focus on what you do have as opposed to what you don't have.

Incorporating Worship: Make each day count; it's a gift from the creator. Nurture your relationships with friends and family by spending quality time with them. Dig the well of faithfulness. Live, laugh, dance, and enjoy life every day. Remember God answers prayers not complaints, so "BE- LIEVE FOR IT!"

Adopting a healthy lifestyle has become a way of life for me. I am a non-smoker, I manage my blood pressure regularly, and through routine bloodwork, I monitor my cholesterol levels. I never add salt to my food, and I stopped drinking sodas. I also eat lots of fruit and veggies and most importantly, I try to avoid stressful situations.

REFLECTIONS

What have you had to persevere through, and how did you do it?

_____

_____

_____

_____

_____

_____

_____

_____

_____

_____

_____

_____

_____

_____

_____

_____

_____

_____

_____

_____

_____

More Dramatic Changes

In 2017, the owner of the property, United Therapeutic, decided to rede-velop the entire block of offices on Spring Street. They gave all of the tenant companies three months to find new space. I was devastated. After several years of having a successful shop again, seven years to be exact, here came the unexpected, and my life was in for another dramatic change. I immediately started looking for a new space. I hoped to find another studio as perfect for me as the one was on Spring Street.

However, before I could settle on a new space for my design studio, I was diagnosed with Multiple Myeloma, a type of bone marrow cancer. I had an appointment with a knee surgeon to have my knees checked out. The surgeon referred me to a hematologist to see why I was so anemic. As it turned out, there it was, the "C" word, cancer.

This type of cancer is not curable. The prognosis, according to the doctors, was the best I could hope for was remission. I started treatment immedi-ately. At first, I believed that I had reached the end of my artistic life as a jewelry designer. But by the grace of God, a stem cell transplant, wonder-ful doctors, the loving support of my loving husband Bill, my sister Diane, and my son Damian, they all helped me to eventually achieve remission, which I am still in today. Bill was my rock who had seen me through the stroke and the cancer diagnosis, holding me up spiritually as well as tend-ing to many of my physical needs.

Sadly, in 2019, he passed away unexpectedly from a heart attack. He was on life support for two weeks. I remember a conversation he and I had about being kept alive using life-sustaining equipment and agreed that we didn't want to be kept alive artificially. Although we were in agreement, deciding to remove a loved one from life support is something I wouldn't wish on anyone. That caused a deep internal scar on the inside of me like no other.

However, I feel his presence daily, whispering to me the words, "Continue on your journey." He would speak spiritual blessings into existence, which made me also do the same. Often, creativity is forged in the fires of adver-sity. Scars, anyone?

Depression Raised Its Ugly Head

Losing Bill set me back almost more than the stroke and cancer had done. Again, I was rendered almost helpless. I was lost and deeply depressed by the loss of my beloved. For many months I could not design or finish a piece of jewelry. The pandemic arrived and I was isolated at home. I could not sleep, and I ate very little. Bill had done most of the cooking after he retired while I spent most of my days at the studio.

However, my wonderful friends came to visit and did their best to cheer me up. They brought me meals and spent time with me – but the creative center of my life seemed to have shifted. A different type of paralysis had me in its grip for a couple of years.

REFLECTIONS

Has depression debilitated you after the death of a loved one? If so, how did you overcome it?

_____

_____

_____

_____

_____

_____

_____

_____

_____

_____

_____

_____

_____

_____

_____

_____

_____

_____

_____

My Vision Is My Victory

Fast forward to 2025, and I am back in the game. I pray that the creator will continue to open my eyes and show me the way I should go. A visionary sees things that are not as though they are. As Hebrews 11:13 says, "These all died in faith, not having received the promises, but having seen them afar off were assured of them, embraced them." Vision will give you strength to persevere through rough times. As God's blessings continue to chase me down, a new chapter of my life has just begun.

I am excited to share that I am designing a new jewelry collection, inspired by exotic, beautiful gemstones imbued with the properties of health and healing. While some days, the design process takes longer than before, I have not lost my ability to create. I am undaunted by the continuing physical challenges from the stroke and current cancer diagnosis. However, my vision is my victory.

So, now you are aware that scars can be internal as much as they are external. They can be emotional as much as they are physical. However, you don't have to let them define you. What really counts is how you respond to them. At one point, scars were forming left and right and I didn't know if I was coming on going. But God has a way of sending Angelic beings in our path, so we don't have to deal with our trials and tribulations alone. Both internal and external scars send a message…that healing has or is taking place. But healing is a choice! I could have easily given up after the stroke, the loss of my studio, the death of my husband, and last but not least, my cancer diagnosis. But giving up wasn't an option for me and shouldn't be one for you either. I could clearly hear the voices of my mom and husband encouraging me to keep pushing. Things could have easily gone another way…BUT GOD, who is rich in mercy and who clearly is not done with me yet.

I only have one life to live. So, every day I try to live my best life and focus on the positive. I believe that when we cannot see our future, it means we must do what we can do as long as we can. God is moving us from where we are to where He wants us to be.

I am not defined by my limitations. God's provisions are always greater than our needs. Even if you can't move a mountain, you can definitely start to shift a few stones. While you cannot change your past, you can rewrite the rest of your life. So, live your life in color!

REFLECTIONS

My Vision:

_____

_____

_____

_____

_____

_____

_____

_____

_____

_____

_____

_____

_____

_____

_____

_____

_____

_____

_____

_____

_____

Bio

Elaine (Elena) Crusoe Aiken

Elena Crusoe Aiken is a celebrated jewelry artist. She grew up in South Carolina, and graduated from secretarial school in Washington, D.C., where she also took business and paralegal courses, landing a job in a law firm where she worked for 20 years. Elena is a widower, and a mom to one son.

She has been making beautiful jewelry designs since the 1990's, using gemstones and other natural materials. Her jewelry has been exhibited in Milan, Italy, Pretoria, South Africa, Costa Rica, in Smithsonian Gift Shops, and in all six Nordstrom locations in the Eastern Region of the United States.

To connect with Elena:

Email: eln0148@aol.com
Website: www.elenadesignstudio.com
Cell: 240-305-8282

www.ingramcontent.com/pod-product-compliance
Lightning Source LLC
Chambersburg PA
CBHW071340130626
46556CB00004B/1958